# Science investigations through stories:

## a blended approach with maths and English

First published 2021 by The Association for Science Education.

The Association for Science Education
College Lane
Hatfield
AL10 9AA

The right of Andy Markwick to be identified as the author of this work has been asserted in accordance with the Copyright, Designs and Patent Act 1988.

Artwork by Georgia Nixon aged 14 years and Lexi Archer aged 5 years
All other images sourced from Shutterstock and Pixabay

Typesetting and design by Karen Dyer

Printed and bound in Great Britain by Printed Easy, Letchworth

ISBN 9780863574757



British Library Cataloguing in Publication Data
A catalogue record for this book is available from the British Library

# Acknowledgements

I would like to thank my primary colleagues and their pupils for trialling these resources so enthusiastically and for suggesting ideas that have helped to ensure that activities are engaging and effective in the classroom.

Special thanks go to Indira Markwick (my wife), and Karen Dyer and Jane Hanrott (ASE) for their proofreading skills and supportive suggestions.

# Contents

# Health & Safety

It is always important to assess any risks that might exist with activities your children take part in. A great place to find this information is the ASE's Be Safe publication. If your institution becomes a member of CLEAPSS of SSERC (Scotland) you will be able to access outstanding Health and Safety support.

As a general safety precaution for activities that involve water or other liquids, ensure that any spills are quickly mopped up to reduce the risk of slipping! Do not use water or other liquids near electrics.

All resources suggested in the activities in this book are readily available in primary schools.

# Introduction

Each activity in this book begins with a short, thought-provoking story that sets the scene for a highly engaging investigation and provides opportunities for children to work scientifically and recall and apply their knowledge of English and mathematics to solve problems.

Children are encouraged to ask questions, observe phenomena closely, manipulate equipment, measure quantities, collect and record data. Working together they will communicate their ideas with others, articulate and justify their conclusions using their own observations and data.

The activities are supported by teachers' notes for each subject suggesting what the children might do and setting a series of challenges.

This learning methodology is novel and creative and provides an effective approach to deepen and assess children's understanding of science, English and mathematics.

The activities presented in this book have been created and trialled over several years with the support of teachers, TAs and pupils in over 40 primary schools. The activities can be used as suggested or very easily adapted for your own classes and learning contexts.

# A lucky escape in Old Oak Wood

Autumn had finally arrived and the trees had become skeletons of their former selves. They were preparing for winter and slowly falling into a deep sleep.

Lily awoke to feel a cool, misty breath engulf her exoskeleton.

As the sun began to rise, beams of light hugged the oak trees, first touching their tips and then slowly seeping down their trunks to reveal a forest blanket, aflame in reds and yellows.

The wind and the leaves danced together, creating a ballet of crimson and gold – it was a spectacular sight to see.

It was time for Lily's journey to begin and this, also, is where her story begins.

At this time of year, Lily always visited her grandmother, who lived at the far side of the wood in an area called Brimble. It was quite a distance and would take Lily several hours to walk, even with her eight legs!

As usual, Lily packed herself a hearty meal and placed it in her rucksack before setting off on her journey.

She decided to take the well-trodden path through the woods. As she walked, each foot met the crisp leaves with a crunch and a crackle. But it wasn't long before the path began to disappear under a thick carpet of wind-blown leaves.

Who knows what was lurking underneath the leaves?

As Lily enjoyed the freshness of the air against her face, her gaze was drawn to the sparse, twinkling canopy high above. There she spied her friend, Lexi, a beautiful dragonfly.

"Hello!" shouted Lily, as loud as she could in order to be heard above the whooshing, whistling wind as it squeezed through the branches of the trees.

"Hello, Lily. Off to see your Grandma?" said Lexi.

Just as Lily was about to say yes, Lexi shrieked…"Watch out for the hole, Lily!"

It was too late. Before Lily could say anything, she was plummeting at an alarming rate.

BUMP! BUMP! BASH! THUMP! OUCH! Lily's abdomen hit the bottom of the hole with a THUD!

Looking up through a chimney-shaped hole, Lily saw Lexi hovering high above.

"Are you OK?" she asked.

"I'm fine I think, Lexi, just a bit sore," moaned Lily.

"Can you climb out?" asked Lexi.

"I don't think so. The hole is too deep and the sides are too steep. Could you lift me out?" replied Lily.

"You're too heavy for me to lift you," said Lexi.

Lexi was right, Lily was too heavy to lift out and there was no one around to help. She was trapped!

Lexi tried to place a twig in the hole for Lily to climb up. But most of the twigs were too short and those that were long enough were too heavy for Lexi to lift.

Then Lexi, who was a rather smart dragonfly, had an idea…

The hole was too deep, the sides too steep and Lily was too heavy to lift. So she thought and thought and thought…maybe she could drop a seed into the hole. The seed would germinate and grow. And, as the stem grew taller and stronger, it would reach the top of the hole and Lily could climb up the stem to freedom and go to see her Grandma!

Lily had enough food to last her for several days and, if she needed more, Lexi could throw food to her.

"What a good idea!" said Lily optimistically.

Lexi and Lily wondered which seed might be the best to use to help Lily to escape from the deep chimney-shaped hole.

***Can you help Lexi and Lily find out?***

# Activities and Questions: Teacher's Notes

## Science

Ask children to discuss what type of animal Lily might be. What evidence do they have from the story? Discuss other animals that have exoskeletons and 8 legs. What is the group name for these animals?

Children could discuss the seasons and in particular autumn. What else happens in autumn? How would we know what season we were in if we didn't have a calendar?

Children could investigate seed germination and growth. Provide children with a selection of seeds (cress, broad bean, mung bean, etc.). Which seed produces a stem that would be long enough (6-8cm) and strong enough for Lily to use to climb out of the hole? Children could check their plant each day and record what they see.

Could children think of any other solutions to Lily's problem?

Children could find out about a woodland habitat. What animals and plants might they find in this habitat?

## Mathematics

Children could measure the dimensions of their chosen seeds (length and width in cm or mm, mass in grams). They could research what seeds require to germinate and, to **challenge** them, they could investigate factors such as temperature, light and moisture, using cress seeds or mung beans. Do seeds grow in the dark? How well will seeds grow in the fridge? Do seeds need water to germinate?

As the seed germinates and grows, children could draw what they see and take measurements, such as numbers of leaves, colours of stem and leaf, etc.

To **challenge** children, they could measure the changing height (cm) of the plants against time (days). The teacher could plot the children's data on a class graph.

## English

Children could write or draw a follow-up story about Lily's journey to her Grandma after she escapes from the hole.

Can children find alternative words for ***engulf***, ***lurking***, ***plummeting***, ***hovering*** and ***chimney-shaped***?

Children could discuss and describe what Lily and Lexi look like. What might Lily's Grandma look like? What would Grandma's house look like?

# Antony and Antonia will go to the party!

"I really enjoy sleeping and the smell of fresh linen," thought April. "My bed is so warm and comfy and it is the weekend, so I can sleep even longer...I don't have to get up!" April hid her head under her duvet and grinned to herself.

But just as April began to fall back to sleep, she was woken, far too early, by a faint 'tap, tap, tap, tap' at her back door.

"Wait a minute," she croaked. "I need to comb my teeth and brush my hair." She was half asleep, you know, and certainly not used to waking up so early at the weekend – who is?

The staircase creaked as April sleepily walked downstairs. She passed Sammy the spider who was busily spinning his daily web. "Good morning, April," said Sammy. "You are up very early."

"Yes, I am," replied April, still half asleep. "Someone is at my back door."

April opened the door to two of her smallest friends, Antony and Antonia, two ants who lived at the bottom of her beautiful garden.

"How are you both on this lovely day?" asked April, through a big yawn.

"We are both very well, thank you for asking. How are you?" replied Antonia.

"Well, apart from having toothpaste in my hair and hair in my teeth, I'm fine, thank you!" replied April.

“We have a favour to ask you,” said Antony.

“Of course!” said April, who was always happy to help anyone. “What favour would that be?”

“Well,” said Antony, “our friends Antoinette and Antario are having a party and we have been invited. We would love to go because we haven’t seen them for such a long time. However, to get there we need to cross the stream at the bottom of our garden. Neither of us can swim well enough to do this. Do you know how we could get to the other side?”

April knew the garden well. She spent much of her time keeping the garden looking beautiful. She loved nothing more than to dig and weed and prune and water her wonderful plants. April prided herself in having the widest range of the most beautiful trees and bushes in the area.

April had an idea…

“Have you ever tried to float across the stream on a leaf?” asked April thoughtfully.

“Never. That sounds great fun!” replied Antonia.

“How would we know which leaf would be safe to use?” asked Antony.

April thought for a moment. “I know some young scientists who may be able to investigate this for you – shall I ask them?”

“Oh, yes please,” replied both Antony and Antonia excitedly.

***Can you help April’s friends to cross the stream?***

# Activities and Questions: Teacher's Notes

## Science

Children could find out which leaf would be best to transport the ants across the river. Provide pupils with a range of leaves (types, sizes, etc.). They could find out the names of the plants that each leaf comes from. Children can plan and carry out an investigation (plan, predict, observe, record, conclude and evaluate)? See below:

| Leaf name | Number of blocks (ants) | If 1 block = 2 ants | If 1 block = 5 ants |
|---|---|---|---|
| | | | |
| | | | |

Take a look at the mathematics section to develop this investigation.

Challenge: **Can you make a boat from aluminium foil?**

What shape is best for the ants?

Provide children with a $10cm^2$ piece of aluminium foil. Can they make a boat that floats? How many blocks or marbles will it carry? Allow pupils to try a range of designs using the same size of foil. Do children use their knowledge gained from using leaves? Do they use tens and ones?

This is an example of scientific modelling.

## Mathematics

Mathematics activities might include counting, addition and unitising.

Float leaves in water (one at a time). How many $1cm^3$ blocks or marbles does it take to sink the leaf? Which leaf would carry most ants?

Pupils could collect the leaves themselves. Are the blocks or marbles the same as ants? What does an ant look like (number of legs, body parts, etc.)?

Tell children that 1 block = 2 ants, or 1 block = 5 ants.

Can they recalculate the number of ants that each leaf was able to carry? *This will be challenging for some children.*

### Challenge

State that one block has a mass of 1g. An ant has a mass of approximately 0.01g. How many ants will each leaf hold?

## English

Encourage children to use, write or say sentences using scientific vocabulary (floating, sinking, naming the leaves). They might like to write a description of their favourite leaf.

Children could discuss what they have discovered. What did they find out (conclusion)?

Children can talk about what they think Antony and Antonia did at the party. What adventures did they have? Children could either write a story, a poem or create a cartoon of Antony's and Antonia's adventures.

# Clumsy Clive

### At breakfast

Clive was first down to breakfast as usual. He was always so very hungry! "He's a growing boy," his mum used to say, especially after Paige, his big sister, called him greedy!

Today was Clive's favourite breakfast, porridge with a trickle of sweet, sweet honey. "Yum, yum, porridge in my tum," said Clive gleefully.

Just as Clive was reaching for his orange juice, he was distracted by Poppy, the puppy, who was chasing her tail. It was such a funny thing to watch.

SPLASH! It was too late – there was juice all over the table, and some on Paige.

"Oh Clive, you are so clumsy sometimes!" barked his mum. "What a mess, Clive. This is not going to be easy to clean up – it is so sticky!"

"My dress is soaking wet. I'm going to need to change, thanks to you!" said Paige angrily.

"Sorry mum, sorry Paige," replied Clive.

## At breaktime

After a morning of really cool maths, it was breaktime. Time for milk. Clive loved his milk, but not as much as being outside with his friends.

In a rush to join his friends at play, his beaker slipped from his hand and CRASH! It fell onto the floor, spilling milk all over the classroom carpet.

"Oh Clive, you are so clumsy sometimes!" sighed Mrs Barrett, his teacher.

"Sorry Mrs Barrett," replied Clive, with a guilty look on his face.

## At lunchtime

The bell rang and it was time for Clive to finish playing catch and get ready for his English lesson. In the lesson, Clive learned about nouns and verbs and strange things called adverbials. It was a great lesson and time just flew by. Before he knew it, it was lunchtime.

Clive could smell dinner and thought, "Bangers and mash with lots of gravy, yum, yum!"

He was right, bangers and mash it was, and flooded with gravy.

Just as Clive was about to pour gravy onto his juicy bangers and fluffy white mash, he glimpsed an aeroplane flying high in the sky.

You guessed it.

Clive spilt gravy all over the table and on his shirt sleeve!

"Oh Clive, you are so clumsy sometimes!" said Olivia, his best friend, who also got gravy on her shirt. "You should carry a cloth around with you," she added thoughtfully.

"What a good idea," replied Clive.

It was science in the afternoon and Mrs Barrett had an idea. What if Clive could investigate which cloth would be the best for him to carry around?

***Can you help Clive to find out which cloth would be best to use to mop up his spills?***

# Activities and Questions: Teacher's Notes

## Science

Children could investigate a range of materials for absorbency (they may also want to make the test a fair one).

There are many ways to do this; tried and tested ways include:

**A.**

1. Cut out a small piece of material so that it fits into a funnel.
2. Place the funnel into a measuring cylinder.
3. Slowly pour 20ml of water onto the material. Children like to use a dropper to do this.
4. Measure how much water travels through the material and into the measuring cylinder. The more water that travels through, the less efficient the material is at absorbing water.

This technique can be adapted to suit the level of ability of your students.

**B.**

1. Pour 10ml of water into a polystyrene chip tray.
2. Cut out a piece of material and place this into a polystyrene chip tray.
3. Leave the material in the tray for 20 seconds.
4. Remove the material and measure how much water is left in the tray. The more water there is left in the tray, the less efficient the material is at absorbing water.

**C.**

1. Using a pipette, squirt some water onto a table.
2. Compare how well different materials soak up the water spill.

Discuss what children discovered and which material would be fit for purpose.

## Mathematics

Children could measure volumes (ml) and times (s). They could measure and cut out agreed sizes of material (surface areas).

## English

Children could discuss their results and then produce a leaflet that would convince Clive about a particular material to use.

Children could write or draw an account of their investigation. They could record their results in a table. What did they find out?

Children could discuss other uses for cloths and decide which materials would be best to use for different purposes. What types of materials are used at home and for what purpose?

# Liar, liar, pants on fire!

Peter lived in the very small, green village of Rilaton in Cornwall. Rilaton is hidden deep in the countryside and only has 100 inhabitants (and this includes all the pets!).

Peter's family had recently moved into the area from the city, because they wanted a healthier life.

Peter had made a few friends, but they were beginning to get rather annoyed with his tales and exaggerations. He was known by the villagers as a 'boy who would stretch the truth a little' and his friends were not amused!

This story is all about Peter's tales and it's up to you to decide whether he was telling the truth, exaggerating or lying.

## Story one

Monday was such a gloriously warm, sunny day that Peter decided to ride his brand new black-and-red bike to school. He made sure that he wore all the correct safety clothing and had passed his cycling proficiency test.

"Good morning," Peter said to his friends as he locked up his bike.

"Good morning, Peter," replied his friends.

"What a nice bike, I love the colour," said Gail.

"It looks like a fast bike to me," added Michael.

"It's the fastest bike in school," said Peter rather confidently. "I was doing over 40mph on my way to school today and I wasn't scared at all. I even overtook a car!"

"Oh Peter, I don't believe you," said Tino. "No one could cycle that fast on a pushbike," added Michael.

"Liar, liar pants on fire!" shouted Tino, Gail and Michael.

"But it's true!" exclaimed Peter.

***What do you think? Was Peter telling the truth, exaggerating or lying?***

## Story two

Tuesday was Sports Day at Peter's school. Children were very excited and ready to take part in running and jumping, all except Peter, who had a sore knee. He had fallen off his bike the day before and was limping rather badly.

"It's a shame I can't run in the races today because I can run like a cheetah," he bragged. "I would win all the races, you know."

"Oh, Peter, I don't believe you," said Michael. "A cheetah can run faster than any other animal. You could not run like a cheetah!"

"Liar, liar pants on fire!" sang the children.

"But it's true!" exclaimed Peter.

***What do you think? Was Peter telling the truth, exaggerating or lying?***

## Story three

At weekends the village children often visited Fred the farmer. Fred always allowed the children to scrump apples from his orchard. When McKenzie, Francesca and Oscar arrived at the orchard, they saw Peter munching on a large red, juicy apple.

“Hello, Peter,” said McKenzie. “What a really nice, red apple!”

“It’s the best apple from the tree. I had to climb to the top of the tree to pick it,” replied Peter.

“I don’t believe you, Peter,” said Francesca. “This tree is far too tall for you to climb to the top.”

“Liar, liar pants on fire!” shouted Oscar, Francesca and McKenzie.

“But it’s true!” exclaimed Peter.

***What do you think? Was Peter telling the truth, exaggerating or lying?***

**Story four**

The weekend had come at last and the village children were making their way to the boating lake to watch the annual boat race and to have a swim. Peter's friends had changed into their swimming costumes and were ready for a dip in the lake.

"I can swim like a fish," said Peter.

"That's not true, is it, Peter?" asked Olivia.

"I would show you, but I've forgotten my swimming trunks today," replied Peter.

"I don't believe you, you are always telling lies," said Tino.

"Liar, liar pants on fire!" sang Peter's friends.

"But it's true!" exclaimed Peter.

Just as the children were about to enter the water, they heard a terrible scream and a loud splash coming from the centre of the lake. A young girl had fallen out of a boat and was struggling to swim to the shore.

She needed help, now!

No one moved, no one said anything. There was a deafening silence.

Then, suddenly, there was a splosh and a splash. Someone was swimming very fast towards the girl. When they reached the girl, they gently held her head above water and swam safely back towards the shore.

Who could this be, thought the children?

It was Peter – he **could** swim like a fish!

Peter had saved the girl's life.

"Well done, Peter!" exclaimed his friends.

***What do you think now? Could Peter have been telling the truth all along?***

# Activities and Questions: Teacher's Notes

## Science

Children could design, build and test the fastest vehicle that they can.

Children could investigate what shapes make the best boat:

- Make a variety of shapes using plasticine (using the same amount of plasticine for each shape)
- Fill a bowl with water
- Drop a shape in the bowl and see how well it floats

Repeat with different shapes.

### Challenge

Children could design, build and test a device that can pick up an apple and raise it to 1 metre above the ground without dropping it.

## Mathematics

Children could measure distances and heights (cm, m) and times (s, min).

## English

Peter became the local hero. Children could write a story describing how this made Peter feel. They could also draw Peter's happy face.

Children could write or draw an article for the local newspaper about the bravery shown by Peter.

# Leaf parachute!

Gail awoke feeling the Sun's rays bathe her in warmth. It was such a glorious day. The Sun was shining and made everything look brand new. It was Sunday morning and, as usual, Gail had her breakfast (the most important meal of the day, her father said), washed, brushed her teeth and combed her hair. She was now ready for a day in the park.

As usual, Gail made herself comfy on a carpet of lush green grass and rested her back against a majestic old oak tree. She had just settled into reading her favourite story, which was all about bugs, when right before her eyes she saw a small spider dangling on a thread. The spider had a pink, almost purple, body and eight dark blue legs. It was quite beautiful, she thought.

The spider was looking straight at her with its compound eyes and, just as she was about to get back to reading her book, she heard, "Hello there, don't be frightened, I won't hurt you. I'm Sammy. I am so glad you like my tree".

Gail wasn't sure, but thought she might have let out a very small scream – not because she was scared of the spider, but because it had spoken to her!

Sure enough, it WAS a speaking spider and, in a small squeaky voice, he said, "I have lived in this wonderful oak tree all my life. My sister Sally lives in a hidden hole deep in the roots of the tree. Every day I like to visit her to sip tea and have a chat about our day. To reach my sister, I must lower myself to the ground using a silk thread".

"That sounds like really hard work to me," said Gail.

"It certainly is," replied Sammy. "And I'm not getting any younger! It takes ages to get to the ground and it can be quite tiring. My friends who live in other trees in the park also need to get to the ground to see their families."

"It would be wonderful to have another way to reach the ground," he added.

Gail thought for a moment and then had an idea…

"Have you ever tried to float to the ground using a leaf?" she asked thoughtfully.

"No, that sounds a really good idea, but which leaf would be best for myself and my friends? We all live in different types of tree," said Sammy, very excitedly.

"I'm not sure, but I know some scientists who could find out for you," replied Gail.

***Can you investigate which leaf would be best to carry Sammy and his friends to the ground?***

# Activities and Questions: Teacher's Notes

## Science

Children could investigate which leaves are best at floating to the ground for Sammy. The leaf must not crash to the ground, it must not turn over and it should fall close to the tree and not float far away.

To **challenge**, children could learn about air resistance and surface area. Do the leaves with larger surface areas fall more slowly? Children should also name the tree that each leaf comes from.

## Mathematics

Children could take measurements such as distance (m, cm) and time (s). They might also want to estimate surface area ($cm^2$) of the leaves using squared paper. This could be used to explain the differences in floating times (s, min).

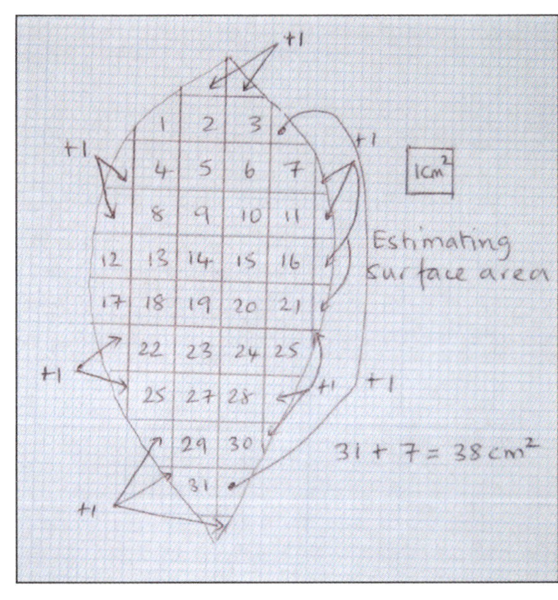

## English

Children could write or draw their account of their investigation.

Children could write a story about the fun that Sammy and his friends had floating to the ground on a leaf.

Children could role-play parts of the story, or adaptations of the story.

# Make a wish

Well, our story begins many years ago, in a mystical world far, far away, where the sky is always beautifully blue, with the occasional floating woolly-white cloud, and the sea is wonderfully warm and a tempting turquoise colour.

Hidden deep in the lush emerald green Derowan Forest lived Lexi, a very, very wise woman. She was the guardian of Derowan Forest and some thought that she was a sorceress with magical powers.

Now, many years had passed and the legend of Lexi, the Wise Woman, had faded from people's memories. Some had not even heard of her!

However, this was not true for Lily.

When Lily was a little girl, she was fascinated by her grandfather's tales of the Wise Woman and how she was able to transform herself into anything she wanted. To keep an eye on the Forest, Lexi would become a powerful eagle and soar high into the sky. Using her amazing sight, nothing would escape her gaze. To scare away people who wanted to harm the Forest, Lexi would transform into a huge, scary grizzly bear, or a fearsome tiger.

Lily was particularly interested in one story, which told of a special dragon's potion that could make a wish come true.

The potion required three ingredients: a fragment of a dragon's brain, a dribble of dragon's sneeze and a drop of a dragon's tears.

Lily was determined to make the potion so that her wish might come true, but to get these ingredients Lily needed a dragon!

Well, luckily, Lily's grandfather knew of a very friendly dragon called Leo. Unlike most dragons who live in fiery caves or deep underneath mountains, Leo lived in a beautiful church spire in a sleepy village called Lanivet. Lily's grandfather was on good terms with the dragon and so it wasn't very long before Lily met Leo.

"Hello, little girl," boomed Leo. "What brings you to my home?"

"Hello, Leo! My name is Lily, and my grandfather said you might be able to help me," said Lily hesitantly.

"And how can I help you, Lily?" enquired Leo.

"Have you heard of Lexi the Wise Woman, and of her magic potion that can make wishes come true?" asked Lily.

"Indeed I have," said Leo, raising an eyebrow. "I take it that you need a slither of my brain, some sneeze and some tears?"

"Yes!" said Lily. "Would that be OK?"

"Well, you may be in luck," grinned Leo.

Dragons can live for thousands of years, as you know. However, few people know that this is because they have hundreds of brains and, when one is old, they just replace it with a new one.

"I could give you a fragment of one of my spare brains, but I will need something in return," said Leo, gazing at Lily's neck. "Is that a gold chain I see?"

"Yes, it was a present from my grandfather", said Lily.

"I remember it and your grandfather well," replied Leo. "I will give you a slice of one of my spare brains for that chain."

Lily didn't want to part with her chain, as it meant so much to her, yet she also needed the slice of dragon's brain for her magic potion.

After what seemed like several minutes of 'umming' and 'aahhing', Lily reluctantly said, "Ok, you have a deal."

"I have a really nasty cold at the moment and so could give you some sneeze. However, I don't think I can give you any tears," said Leo.

Lily thought hard. She had to make Leo cry! She didn't want to be nasty and make Leo sad. How could she make Leo cry without making him sad? Then Lily had it!

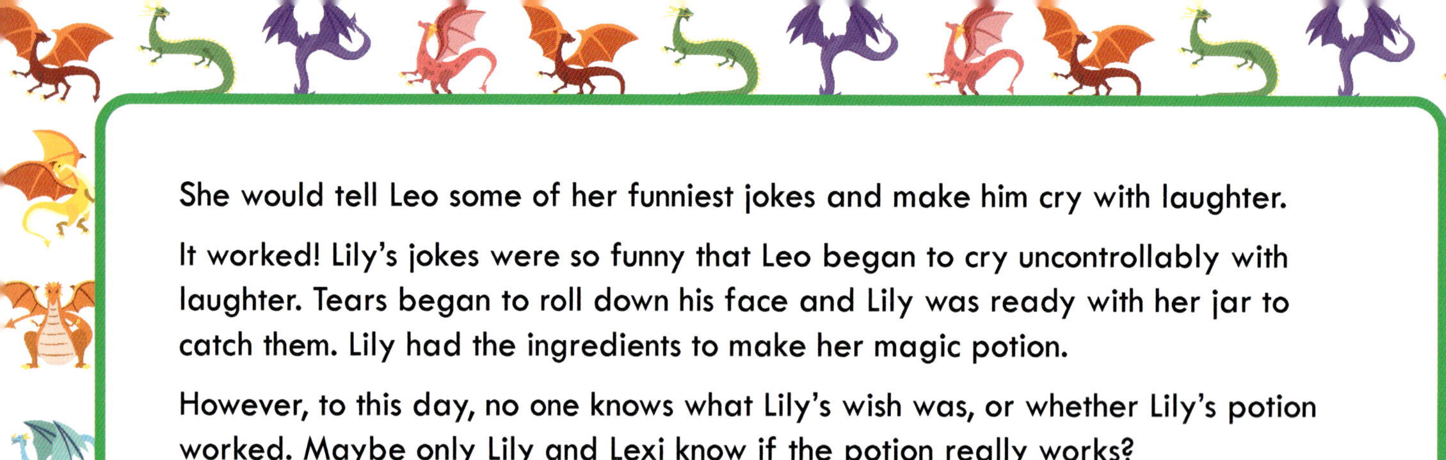

She would tell Leo some of her funniest jokes and make him cry with laughter.

It worked! Lily's jokes were so funny that Leo began to cry uncontrollably with laughter. Tears began to roll down his face and Lily was ready with her jar to catch them. Lily had the ingredients to make her magic potion.

However, to this day, no one knows what Lily's wish was, or whether Lily's potion worked. Maybe only Lily and Lexi know if the potion really works?

***Would you like to make the dragon's potion?***

# Activities and Questions: Teacher's Notes

## The magic recipe

1. 65ml Dragon's tears
2. 7.5ml juice of Dragon's brain
3. 55ml Dragon's sneeze

### The Wise Woman once said

"If the **red** is on top and the yellow on the bottom, then and only then will your wish come true."

## Science

Children will explore the natural phenomena of immiscibility (oil and water do not mix). Children can be shown that red cabbage juice is blue in water (neutral) and red in acid (vinegar).

Children will learn the names of scientific equipment and practice using them. It is suggested that they are given a measuring cylinder, funnel, syringe, pipette, and beaker.

See the mathematics section to see how science can be made quantitative.

### Method

1. Cut up the red cabbage into small pieces using scissors.
2. Place the red cabbage into a small beaker or cup and add enough cold water to cover the cabbage. Stir this for a few minutes with a spoon. **Before adding the water** ask children what colour they think the red cabbage will change the water. (Most will say red or purple – but it is blue!). This is juice of Dragon's brain!
3. This solution is an indicator. It is red in acid and blue in neutral solutions like water.
4. Using a measuring cylinder and a funnel transfer the Dragon's tears into the Magic potion bottle. Remember that the tears are made of distilled malt vinegar, so be careful not to get this in your eyes. If you do, wash your eyes with tap water!
5. Using a 5ml syringe transfer the juice of Dragon's brain from the beaker into the magic potion bottle. **Before adding the juice of Dragon's brain,** ask children what colour they think the Dragon's tears will change to.
6. Using the same measuring cylinder ask children to carefully transfer the dragon's sneeze into the Magic potion bottle (This is the vegetable oil!). What happens? Can they make the red float on top and the yellow on the bottom? Can you?

## Mathematics

Children could use this activity to practice addition and measure volumes in mls. They could estimate volumes and decide which volume is the greatest. The volumes used could be altered to provide challenge for children. Ask children what the total volume of liquid in the potion bottle is or what the volume of dragon's tears + dragon's sneeze is. What is the total volume of all liquids used in the class? How many filled syringes would it take to measure out 50mls of juice of Dragon's brain?

## English

1. Children could design a colourful leaflet that shows the recipe for making the magic potion.
2. Children could write a poem or song or create a cartoon about the Dragon.
3. Is there another way that Lily could have made Leo cry, without upsetting him (tickle)? Re-write this part of the story but include your idea.
4. Children could role-play part or all the story.
5. What adjective in the story is the children's favourite? Why?

# Mother knows best

**Monday**

It was a bright, sunny Monday morning. The sun squeezed through the clumps of leaves to nudge awake Cobby, a bushy-tailed squirrel.

"I'm so hungry," said Cobby, yawning from ear to ear.

"Be patient, young squirrel," said Cobby's mother. "Food will be ready in a jiffy."

Cobby had spied a delicious bunch of hazelnuts on a nearby tree. "Don't worry, Mum, I can get my own breakfast. I could easily jump across to the hazel tree," smiled Cobby.

Cobby's mother was not amused and said sternly, "No, Cobby, it is too far. You will fall and hurt yourself."

Cobby, being Cobby, did not listen to his mother. He felt hungry and thought that he was such a good jumper he could easily reach the hazel tree.

With a run and a jump he flew through the air towards the hazel tree and…crunch…! He had only just made it, but had landed awkwardly, twisting his foot, and it was VERY painful.

"Oh dear, Cobby, what did I say?" scolded Cobby's mother.

***What should Cobby have done?***

**Tuesday**

Tuesday afternoon was wet, very wet, and Cobby and his mother were foraging in the wood for nuts and berries.

As they walked through the wood, Cobby began to splash in all the puddles.

"I don't think you should do that, Cobby. You will get wet and may catch a cold if you are not careful," warned Cobby's mother.

Cobby, being Cobby, did not listen to his mother and splashed and sploshed in every puddle that he could find.

But one of the puddles was deeper than the others. When Cobby jumped into this puddle, first his legs, then his tummy, then his shoulders disappeared. This was a deep puddle. Cobby was drenched!

"Oh dear, Cobby, what did I say?" said Cobby's mother sternly.

***What should Cobby have done?***

**Wednesday**

Wednesday was a cold damp day and Cobby and his mother were collecting mushrooms for dinner. Cobby's mother was careful to show him which mushrooms were safe to pick.

"Only pick these mushrooms," said Cobby's mother. "The others may be poisonous."

Cobby, being Cobby, did not listen to his mother. He found some mushrooms that were the same shape as, but a different colour from, the ones his mother showed him. "They look almost the same, so how can these hurt me?" Cobby thought, as he picked and ate one.

It wasn't long before Cobby began to feel ill and had a very upset tummy.

"Oh dear, Cobby, what did I say?" said Cobby's mother.

***What should Cobby have done?***

**Thursday**

Thursday was a rather blustery day. The breeze lifted leaves into the air and made them dance. It was a wonderful sight to see.

Cobby and his mother were on their way to see Grandma squirrel, but they had to cross a very busy road.

"We must use the bridge to get to the other side," said Cobby's mother.

Cobby, being Cobby, was not paying attention and did not hear his mother over the howling wind.

He ran, zigzagging across the busy road and, just before he reached the other side, a fast-moving car clipped his tail.

"OUCH!" said Cobby. "That hurt and I've lost some of my bushy tail!"

"Oh Cobby, what did I say?" sighed Cobby's mother. "That was a silly thing to do."

***What should Cobby have done?***

**Friday**

Friday morning was met with warm sunshine.

"What is that on our tree?" asked Cobby, staring at a large yellow, oval-shaped basket.

"That is a wasp nest. Do not get too close. Wasps can sting!" warned Cobby's mother.

Cobby, being Cobby, was far too inquisitive and wanted to have a closer look. After all, he thought rather arrogantly, what could a tiny wasp do to him? He could move much faster than a wasp!

Cobby crept closer and closer to the wasp nest. Just at the point when he could almost touch it, several very angry wasps flew out of the nest and stung his nose.

"OUCH!" The pain was excruciating. He turned and ran home as fast as he could.

"Oh dear, Cobby, what did I say?" said Cobby's mother.

***What should Cobby have done?***

## Saturday

Saturday was a rather dull, wet and cold day. Cobby woke up feeling rather sorry for himself.

"I feel terrible," he thought. "I have a cold, my ankle is swollen, part of my beautiful bushy tail is missing and my nose is very sore. I wish I had listened to my mother!"

"You will need to stay indoors today, Cobby my dear, so that you can recover. Tomorrow we are taking a walk through the woods to see your Auntie," explained Cobby's mother.

## Sunday

Sunday morning was wonderfully bright, yet very cold indeed.

"You must dress up warm today," said Cobby's mother. "The wind is bitterly cold."

Cobby, being Cobby, thought, "my bushy tail will keep me warm, I won't need to."

Then he remembered what had happened to him during the week and thought, "I must listen to my mother." He put on his warm coat.

As Cobby entered the chilly air, puffs of condensation could be seen with every breath that he exhaled. He was very glad that he had listened to his mother. It was VERY cold and he would have been frozen without his coat!

As Cobby and his mother walked along the woodland path, they saw a lake that had frozen over.

"I'm going to skate on the ice," said Cobby excitedly.

"No, Cobby, the ice is too thin and very dangerous," explained Cobby's mother.

Cobby, being Cobby, thought that as long as he tiptoed on the ice he would be ok. Then he remembered what had happened to him during the week and thought, "I must listen to my mother." He stayed well away from the ice.

Just as they headed away from the lake, they heard some children playing with a football. One of the children kicked the football high into the sky and, as it fell, it landed on the ice and CRACK, the ice broke.

"That was a lucky escape!" exclaimed Cobby. " I'm so glad that I listened to you, Mother."

Cobby remembered all the times that he hadn't listened to his mother and thought to himself, **"Mother knows best."**

# Activities and Questions: Teacher's Notes

## Science

Children could describe the habitat of a squirrel. Where might they live? What would they eat? What other animals and plants share this habitat?

Mushrooms are a type of fungus. Children could find out about other types of fungi.

Children could investigate which materials would keep them warm for longest:

- Place some warm water in 3 beakers or cups (same amount of water in each)
- Wrap each container in a different material (same amount of material)
- Measure the temperature of the water in each container every 10 minutes. Which material keeps the water warmest?

NB: Water should not be hotter than 45°C. Do not do this experiment near any electrical equipment.

## Mathematics

Children could measure temperature ($^0C$). They might also like to measure areas ($cm^2$) of material used, to ensure a fair test.

### Challenge

Children could measure the temperature of the water at the beginning and at the end. They could take the lowest temperature away from the highest to obtain the temperature change (HighT - LowT = Tchange). Using scientific notation, this looks like:

$$\Delta T = T_f - T_i$$

## English

Children could choose a day in the story. Rewrite or sketch this part of the story, but add another character.

Children could list some of the nouns, verbs and adverbs used. Can they think of alternative words for these?

Children could choose one of the following words: ***excruciating***, ***inquisitive***, ***arrogantly***. Using the letters, how many different words can they make from each?

# Rockabilly Rat needs a special hat

Saturday had almost arrived, and Rockabilly was an extremely excited rat. Saturday was dance night at the church hall and Rockabilly Rat enjoyed nothing more than to dance and dance and dance!

The church hall was a grey, rectangular brick building and sat next to a gloriously proud church with a tall spire that reached towards the sky.

The hall was about 1.5 kilometres from Rockabilly's home. Rockabilly often walked to the hall, which took him along a winding country road, bounded by tall, thick hedges.

Honeysuckle, hawthorn, dog rose, blackthorn, primrose and strawberry plants grew in the hedge. Birds including sparrows, robins, finches, blackbirds and pigeons acrobatically flapped and foraged amongst the bushes and trees, while butterflies, ladybirds, spiders and ants lived their secret lives hidden deep in the hedge's foliage. In the puddles and ponds lived tadpoles, slowly metamorphosing into frogs.

It was such a wonderful walk, thought Rockabilly, filled with sweet aromas and tuneful birdsong, but the weather forecast for Saturday was not good. It spoke of high winds and rain. This could be a disaster, thought Rockabilly.

"My wonderful quiff will get wet and become flattened. I could not arrive at the dance without my wonderful quiff! I need a hat!" thought Rockabilly Rat.

***Can you help Rockabilly Rat?***

# Activities and Questions: Teacher's Notes

## Science

Children could design and make a hat for Rockabilly Rat. It would need to sit nicely on his head without damaging his quiff and, to stop his hair getting wet, it must be waterproof. How would it be held onto his head and not be blown away in the wind?

What do the plants and animals look like in the story? What other animals and plants might Rockabilly Rat have seen in the country lane?

Children could group the animals in the story, and any others that they add, into arachnid, insect, mammal, reptile and bird.

## Mathematics

Making Rockabilly's hat requires measuring length (cm), width (cm) and the circumference of a head (cm).

### Challenge

Do taller people have larger heads? Children could collect data from members of their class to see if there is a correlation between height and head circumference.

How long would it take to walk 1.5km if Rockabilly walks at 1km every hour (1km/hr)?

Could children find out how many petals are on a primrose, daisy and dog rose? Children can record this information in a table. Does the same type of flower always have the same number of petals? This challenge might be achieved more easily if groups in the class share their data with everyone.

## English

Rockabilly arrives at the dance:

- With a wonderful quiff
- With flattened and wet hair

Children could write or draw an end to the story for each possible scenario.

Children could create a flier (poster) for the Saturday dance.

# Rockabilly Rat needs a special hat - extending the story

Rockabilly's hat worked wonderfully well. He arrived at the dance with a quiff that looked the business!

As soon as he heard the music, Rockabilly leaped onto the dance floor, slipped and fell onto his bottom.

OUCH! "That wasn't supposed to happen," cried Rockabilly Rat, carefully trying to maintain his perfect quiff.

Rockabilly's dancing shoes were wet and so slippery that he couldn't grip the floor enough to dance!

"Oh no! What will I do?" asked Rockabilly. "I need some dancing shoes that will grip the dance floor, even when they are wet!"

***Can you help Rockabilly Rat?***

# Activities and Questions: Teacher's Notes

## Science

Children could investigate a range of materials that might help Rockabilly Rat grip the floor better. The material must be able to grip the floor when wet.

Choose a material that grips the floor well. Attach a Newton meter to the material so that it can be pulled along. How much force is needed to make the material move?

### Challenge

Place a 100g mass onto the material. How much force is needed to move the material now?

If children decide to compare different materials, they could put their data in a table.

NB: The addition of a mass models the weight of a person: the more mass, the greater the person's weight. Do shoes have better grip if the person wearing them weighs more?

## Mathematics

During the investigation, children could:

- measure force using a Newton meter (Force meter)
- place data into a table. Arrange the materials in order of best grip to least grip.

## English

The children could design a web page that will sell these new extra-grip shoes.

The children could rewrite sections of Rockabilly Rat's story, but apply onomatopoeia.

The children could role-play Rockabilly's night out.

# Slippy the Slug

Everyone knows that slugs are slimy...don't they?

Well, this is a story about a very slimy slug called Slippy.

Slippy lived in the undergrowth in a beautiful garden, just underneath the yummy Brussels sprouts.

Slippy was always the first slug to wake up. He just couldn't wait to go into the garden and begin slipping, sliding, skidding and gliding. He played for hours with his friends in the garden, from dawn to dusk.

Slippy was the best skidder in the whole garden, you know! He could even slip and slide and skid and glide faster than Speedy the Spud, who was a champion racing snail!

But early one morning, when Slippy woke up, he couldn't move! He had no slip, he couldn't slide, skid, or even glide...he had no slime!

***What was he going to do?***

Well, Slippy's best friend Boggle Eyes was very concerned. Slippy was always the first in the garden. Where was he? Something must be wrong. "I must go and find Slippy," she muttered to herself.

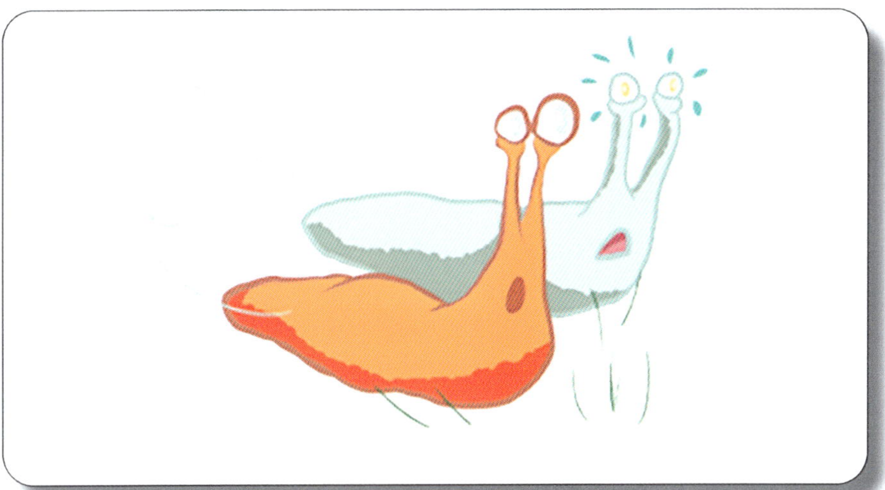

When Boggle Eyes arrived at Slippy's home, just under the yummy Brussels sprouts, she asked, "What is wrong?"

Slippy was sad, and replied, "I can't slip or slide, or skid or glide. I have no slime!"

"Oh dear," said Boggle Eyes. That could be a problem. Then, just as Slippy began to cry, Boggle Eyes shouted, "I have it!"

"Don't worry, Slippy," said Boggle Eyes excitedly. "I know some children who are brilliant scientists. They may be able to help you."

"How can they help me?" asked Slippy.

"Well," replied Boggle Eyes, "they could investigate which liquid would make the slippiest slime for you, so that you could once again slip, slide, skid and glide."

"Wow!" said Slippy. "If they can do that for me, I will be able to have fun with my friends in the garden again! Thank you, Boggle Eyes, you are such a good friend!"

***Can you find a slippery liquid for Slippy the Slug?***

# Activities and Questions: Teacher's Notes

## Science

Children might investigate how slippery different types of liquids are:

- Using a pipette, place some of each liquid onto a tray (a white board works well)
- Carefully place a flat-bottomed glass bead onto each liquid. Gently tilt the tray to see which bead slips the fastest and furthest. Children might want to predict which liquid might be best.

### Challenge

The liquid would need to be safe for Slippy. How could children find out about this? (Good liquids to use might be water, cooking oil, child-friendly liquid soap, honey, tomato sauce, baby shampoo or children's moisturiser.)

## Mathematics

Children could measure time (s) and distances (cm).

### Challenge

Children could be introduced to measuring angles using a protractor.

## English

Children could create a leaflet trying to sell a liquid to slugs who have lost their slime.

Children could discuss what they found out and either write or draw an account of their investigation.

Children could write a section for a sports newspaper or create a cartoon strip showing the Garden Olympic Games.

Children could role-play the Garden Olympic Games.

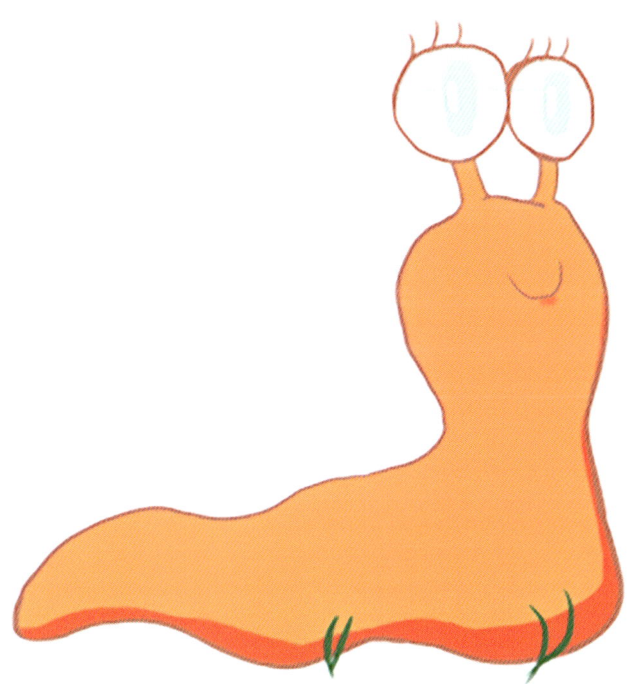

# The lost cargo

Lamorna had just sat down to breakfast when a story on the radio caught her attention.

"It was a lucky escape for the *Cornish Treasure* last night", reported a voice on the radio. "The ferocity of the storm off the coast of Coverack was unbelievable and almost claimed another ship for Davy Jones's locker," the voice continued. "Cyril Peters, you are the lighthouse keeper and were on duty last night. Can you explain what you saw?"

"Well, we could see the *Cornish Treasure* from the lighthouse, and all seemed well. The sea was calm at first. But, without warning, the storm came, and we could see that the *Cornish Treasure* was beginning to get into difficulties. We had to act fast! We sounded the foghorn and shone the lighthouse's light to alert the ship of the perilous rocks it was headed for. We were going to launch the lifeboat but just as quickly as the storm hit, it disappeared and we saw that the *Cornish Treasure* was safe," explained Cyril.

"This just goes to show that the work of our coastguards is so important in saving lives," said the voice on the radio. "I'm turning now to the captain of the *Cornish Treasure*. Captain Pengelly, last night's ordeal must have been terrifying for you and your crew. Can you tell us in your own words how the events of last night unfolded?"

"It was a terrifying and very strange experience. The sea was calm, and the sky was clear and beautifully blue with just a few floating, fluffy clouds and we could hear several seagulls squawking above. And then, from nowhere, we became engulfed in mist and the sea became very rough.

"Waves as high as ten metres began to hit the ship's decks and so I ordered everyone to leave the deck areas and go below. Within a couple of minutes, twenty-metre-high waves were towering above the ship and blocking out the sky. All became dark as waves relentlessly pounded the deck. It was terrifying!

"Thankfully the lighthouse, with its extremely loud foghorn, made me aware that the ship had drifted dangerously close to the jagged rocks near the shore. A collision with these would have ripped the ship apart and we would have been in mortal danger. I had just enough time to steer the ship away from the rocks and to safety.

"As we moved away from the coast, the sea became calmer and the sky once more could be seen. It was as if nothing had happened!

"Casting my eyes over the ship for possible damage, I noticed that our precious cargo had vanished, swept overboard by the huge waves. I can only hope that the cargo has reached the shore and will be found," said Captain Pengelly.

"What cargo is this?" asked the voice.

"We were transporting the fossilised remains of an unknown animal species found buried deep in the remote Welsh mountains. The fossil was going to be analysed and hopefully identified by a team of world-renowned palaeontologists. But unless we can salvage the remains from the coastline, we will never know what the creature was," replied Captain Pengelly.

"Well, let's hope that someone finds the remains washed up on the seashore," said the voice.

Lamorna had been intrigued by the story and began to daydream.

"Wouldn't it be wonderful to find the fossil on the beach so that the scientists could identify the creature? I wonder what the creature could be?" thought Lamorna.

That very day, Lamorna and her friend Tino decided to examine the beach area to see what they could find.

It wasn't too long before Tino discovered a strange-looking object on the beach.

"Is this a fossil, Lamorna?" asked Tino.

"Yes, I think it is," replied Lamorna excitedly.

"Let's look for more," said Tino.

The friends carefully scoured the beach and found several fossil fragments.

Lamorna had taken her camera with her and, as each fossil was found, she took a photograph.

***Lamorna needs your help to identify the creature from the fossils that she and Tino collected. Look carefully at the photographs and answer the questions.***

| Picture of fossil | Dimension/m |
|---|---|
| | Largest spine is 3 |
| | Length is 5 |
| | 0.5 base to point |
| | 0.5 base to point |

***Can you answer these questions?***

1. From the fragments retrieved from the beach, do you think that the remains are of an animal or plant? Explain why you think this.
2. Discuss in your group what you think each fossilised fragment represents and what it might have been used for.
3. What do you think the organism eats? Explain why you think this.
4. Sketch what you think the original animal looked like.
5. What type of habitat do you think it lived in?

***Lamorna and Tino walked around the cliff and this is what they saw!***

***Could there be some truth in the existence of Welsh dragons?***

What do you think?